"MUD IN YER

THE BRITISH COUNTRYSIDE AS NEVER SEEN BEFORE!

By Donald McDonald

DOWN ON THE FARM...

CLUCK MUCK

CLOPPITY PLOPPITY

MULES STOOLS

PIGGY BIGG

MOO POO

DONKEY DOLLOP

ANY BRAND FOR ANY JOB!

P.Y.O. MANURE £1 per bag

"I'M SORRY SOPHIE, BUT IF THIS DON'T WORK THEN BRUTUS GOES TO THE ABATTOIR."

"I KNOWS THEY'RE STUPID FRED COS THEY CRAPS ALL OVER THEIR BREAKFAST!"

"COR DAISY! LOOK AT THE ARM ON THAT!"

"GOD! IT'S LIKE AN AUDITION FOR THE SOOTY SHOW!"

"I SEE THE RECTOR'S BIN ON ONE O' HIS "PASTORAL VISITS" AGAIN!"

"'ERE! TROJAN OLD MATE... GOT ANY OF THEM HAY FLAVOURED CONDOMS LEFT?"

CHOMP!
ROJ!
"MUM! ROGER'S FIGHTING WITH THE SOW JUST LIKE DAD SOMETIMES DOES!"

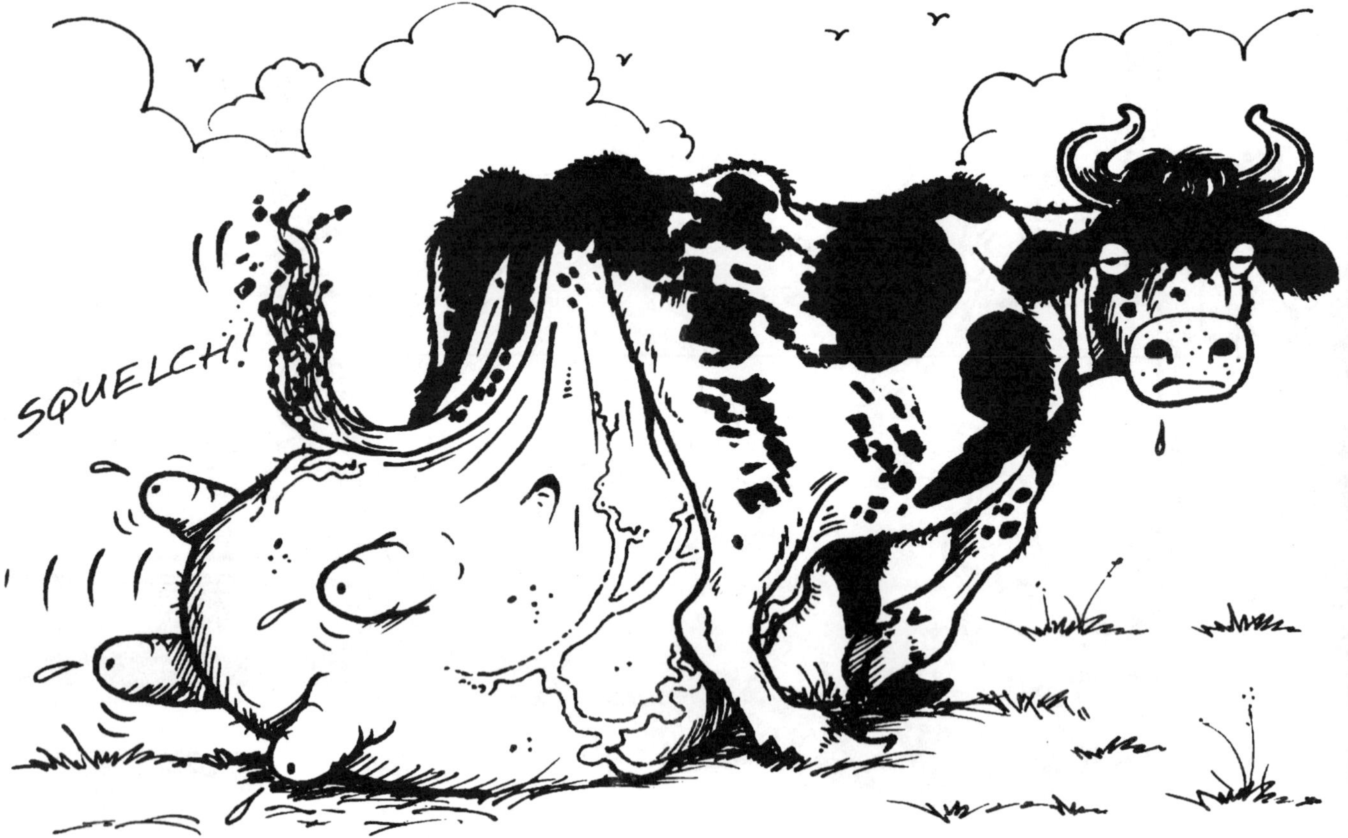

"WHAT A DRAG!"

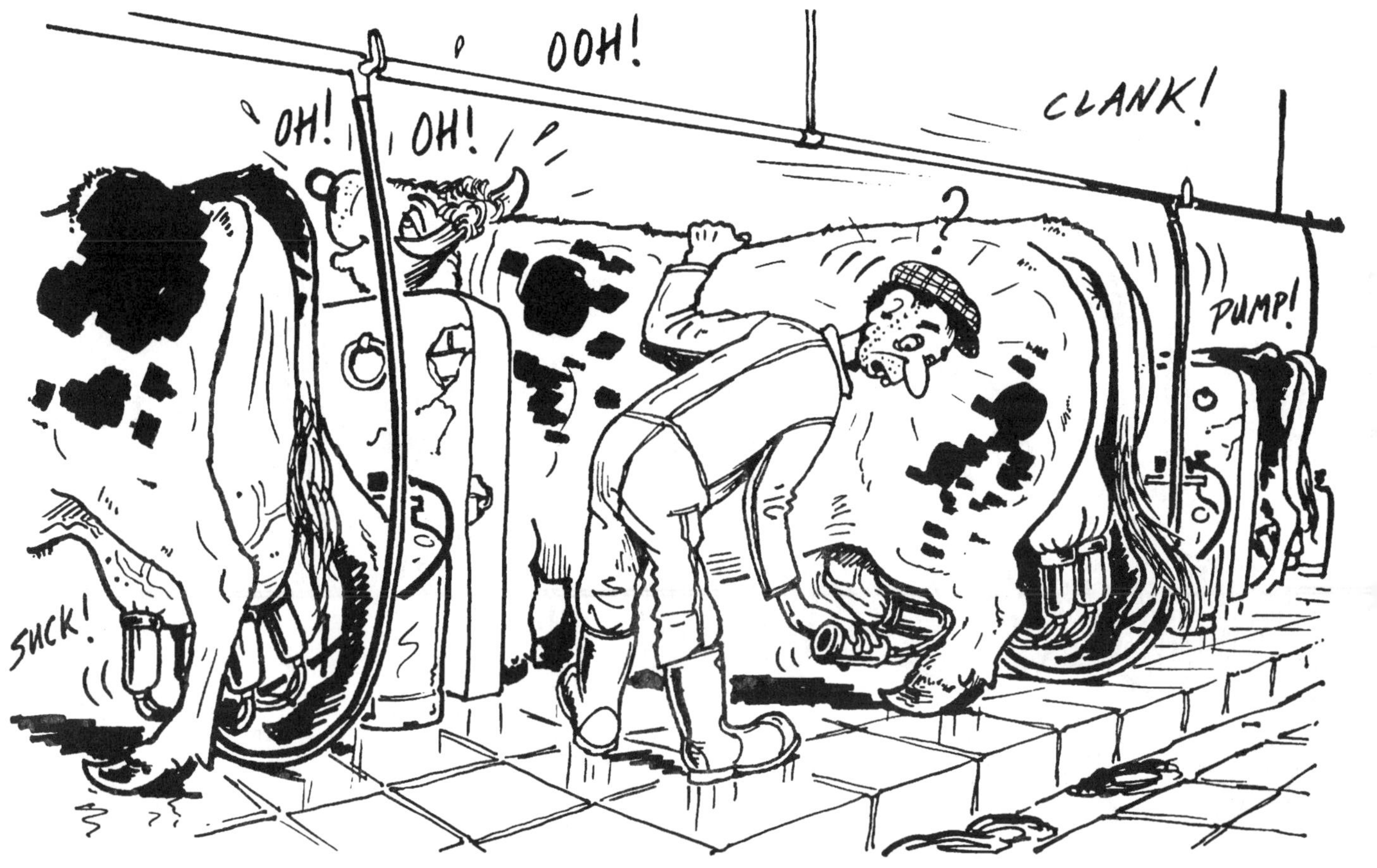

"OOER?"

"IT'S ALRIGHT JON, I THINK HE MISSED US!"

NATURAL HISTORY...

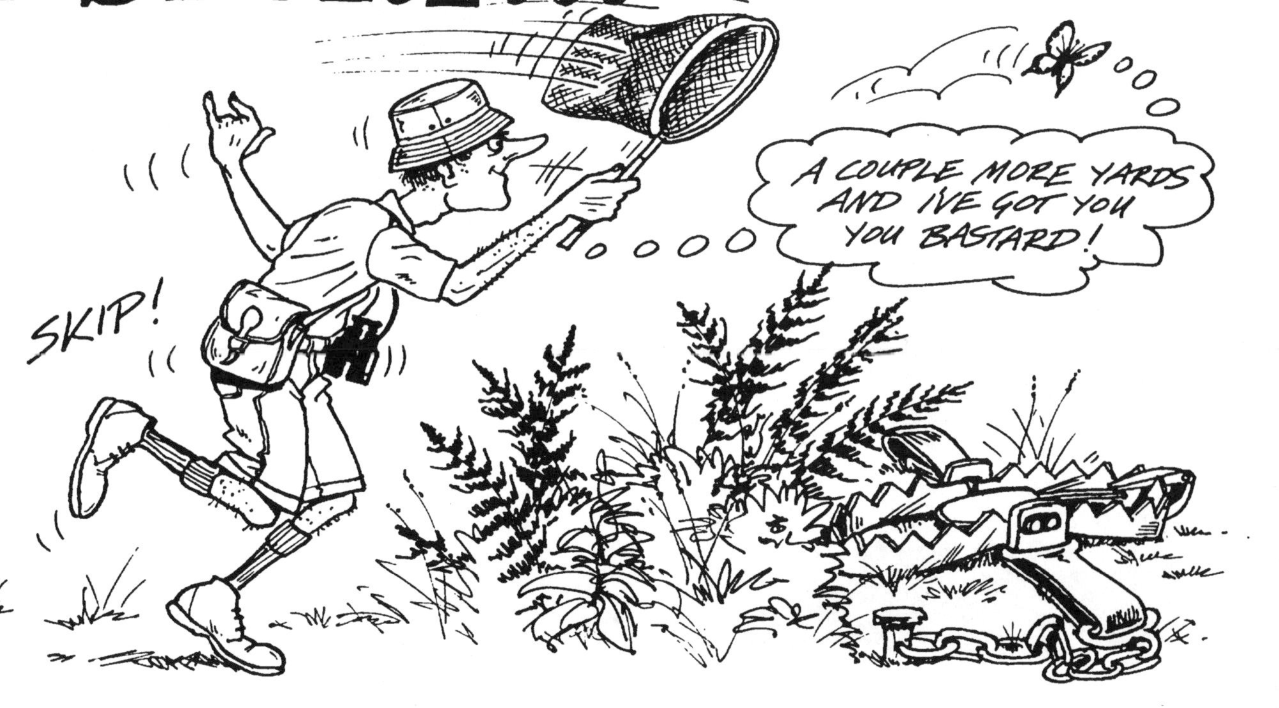

"UH-OH!"

"I'VE GOT NO SYMPATHY IRIS, I'VE WARNED YOU THAT FROO-FROO LOOKS LIKE A SHEEP MORE THAN ONCE!"

"NOW CHILDREN, LAST WEEK WE DISCUSSED HOW WE USE SEX TO BOND OUR RELATIONSHIPS WITH MUTUAL RESPECT AND TRUST .... WELL THIS WEEK WE ARE GOING TO LOOK AT HUMAN SEX!"

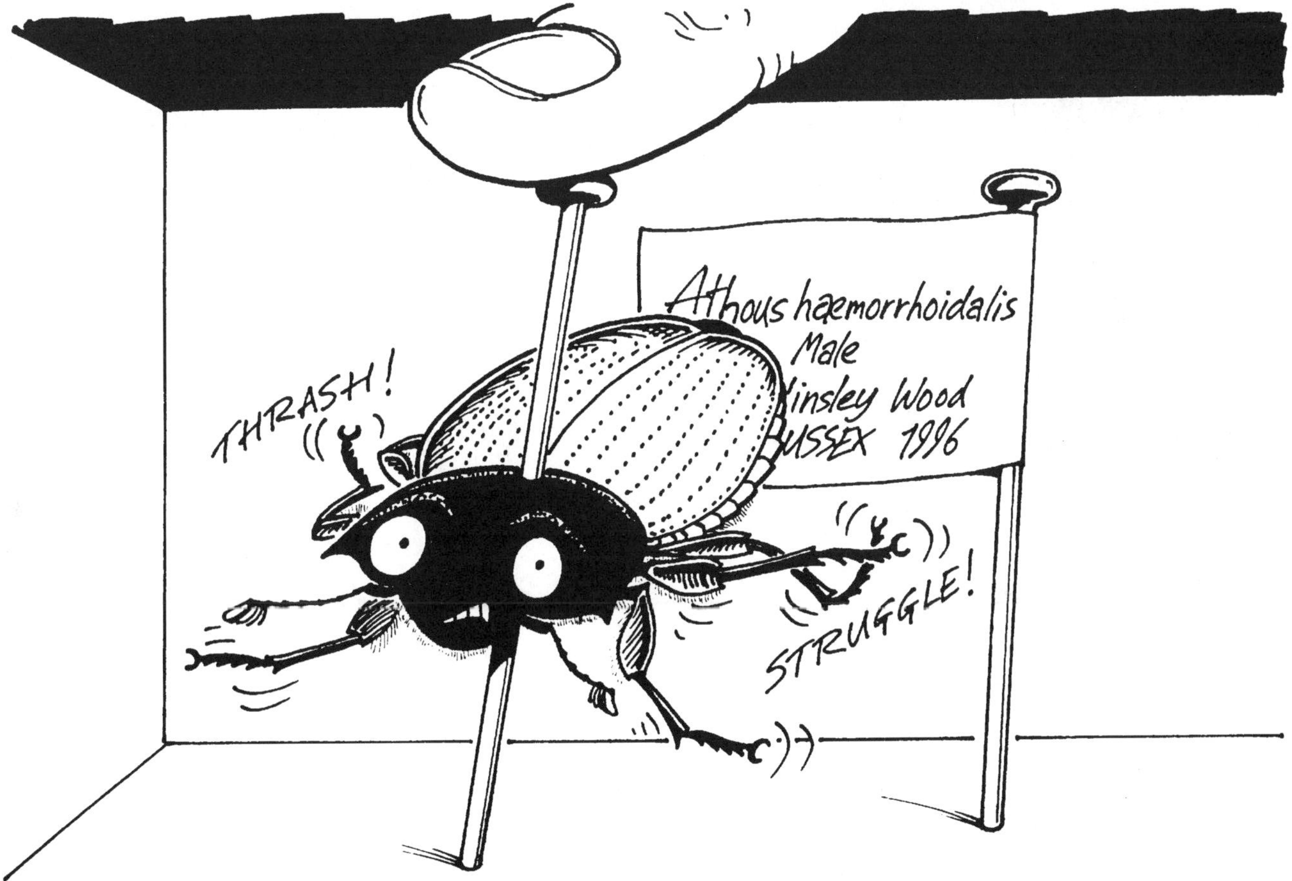

"DO YOU EVER GET THE FEELING YOU'RE NOT GOING ANYWHERE!"

"DON'T ASK QUESTIONS CYRIL...ALL THE NATURE BOOKS SAY WE DO THIS IN AUTUMN.....ALRIGHT!"

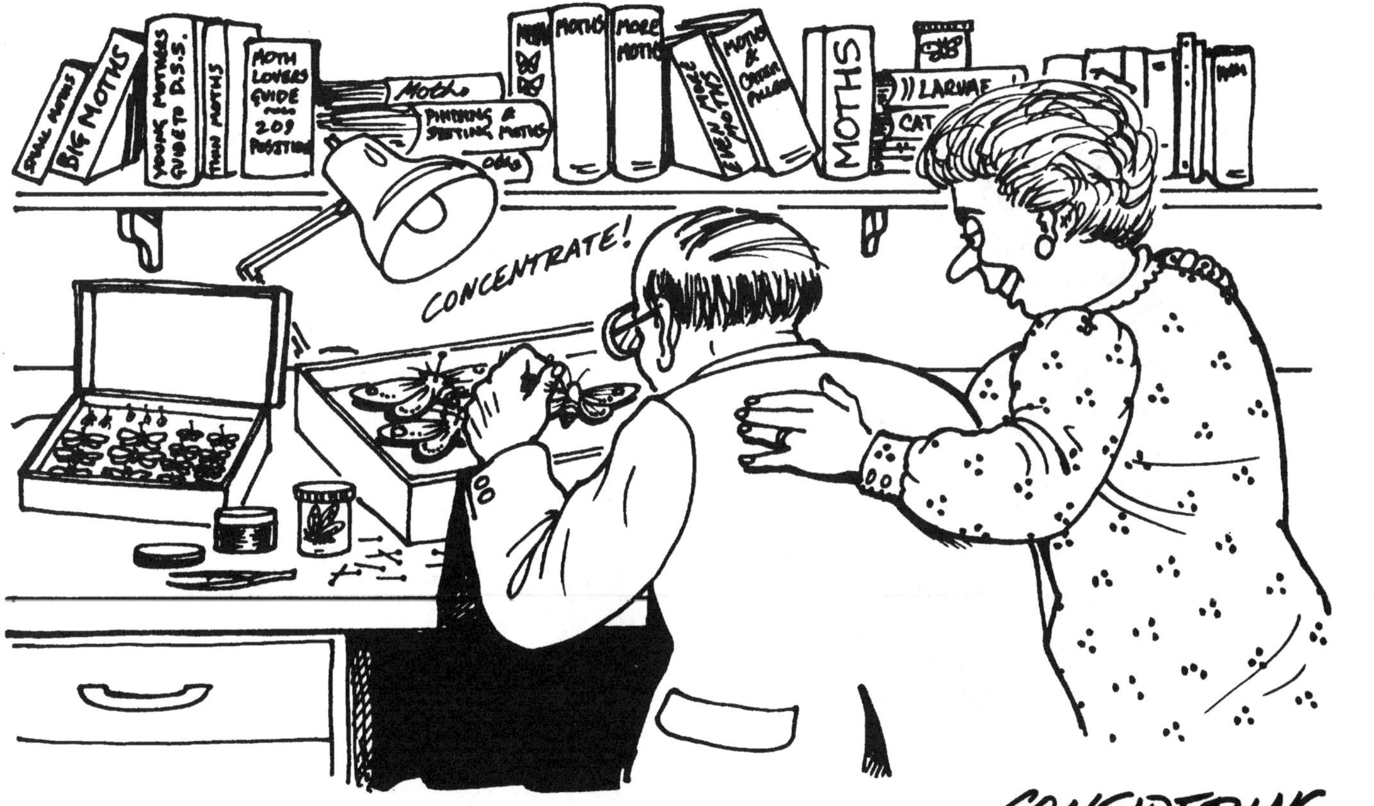

"YES GERALD THEY ARE VERY LIFELIKE.... CONSIDERING THEY'RE ALL DEAD YOU CRUEL BASTARD!"

"THE GAMEKEEPER REPORTED SEEING A PARTICULARLY FINE GROUSE AROUND ABOUT HERE SOMEWHERE!"

"SEE! BEST TIME TO CATCH 'EM IS WHEN THEIR HEADS ARE FULL OF BUSINESS!"

"I MAY BE A TOWNIE TO YOU BUT I KNOW A SPECIES THAT'S NEW TO SCIENCE WHEN I SEE ONE... THAT'S WHAT THIS FROG IS!"

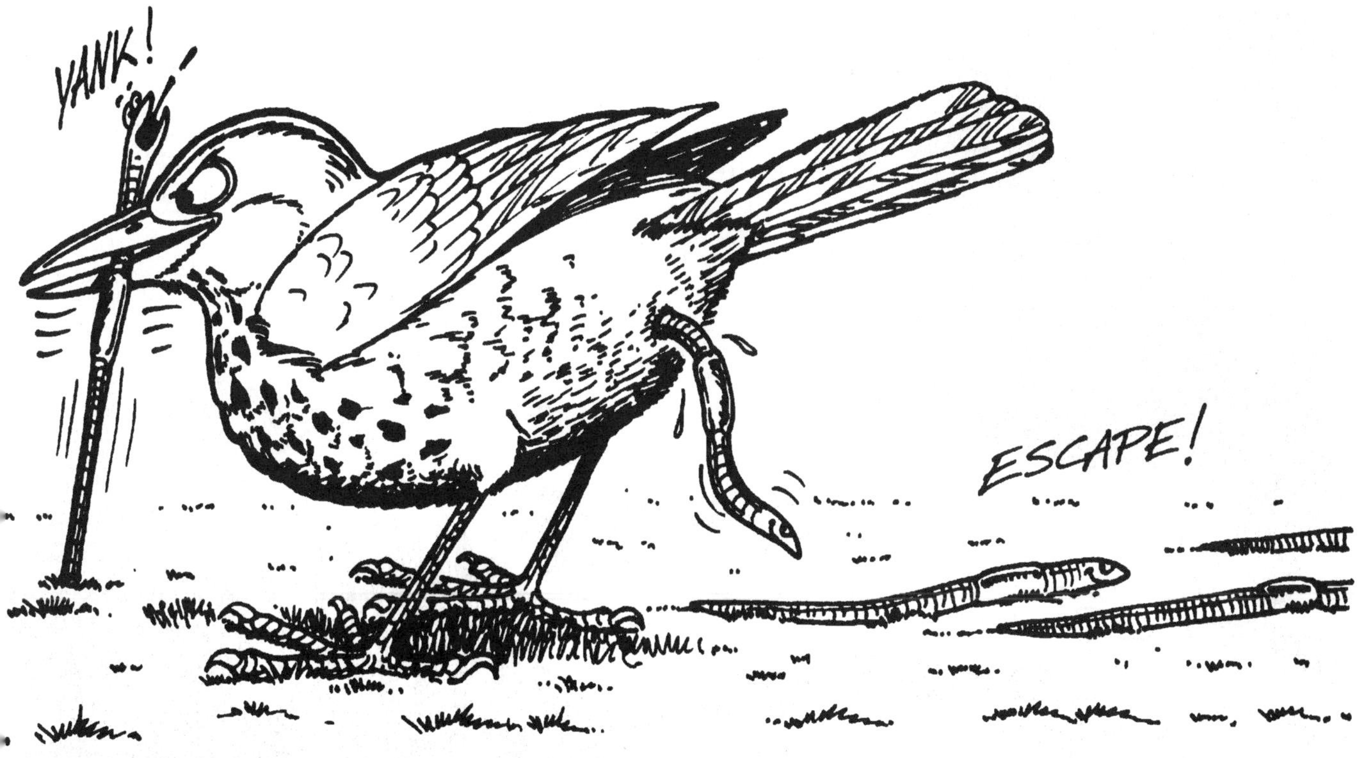

"I'VE BEEN EATING SINCE DAWN AND I'M STILL HUNGRY!"

"HERE HE COMES SON.... PULL IT! PULL IT! IF IT MOVES HE'LL TRY TO RUN IT OVER!"

"ER.. SARGE.. LOSING MY VIRGINITY WITH THAT SHEEP WASN'T QUITE WHAT I EXPECTED!"

"YOU KNOW THIS "RUT" YOU WERE TELLING ME ABOUT DAD... ARE YOU SURE YOU KNOW WHAT YOU ARE TALKING ABOUT!"

TOURISM & OUTWARD-BOUND...

"LISTEN PAL, WE MAY BE A BIT BEHIND THE TIMES ROUND HERE BUT NO, I AIN'T GOT CHANGE FOR A GROAT!"

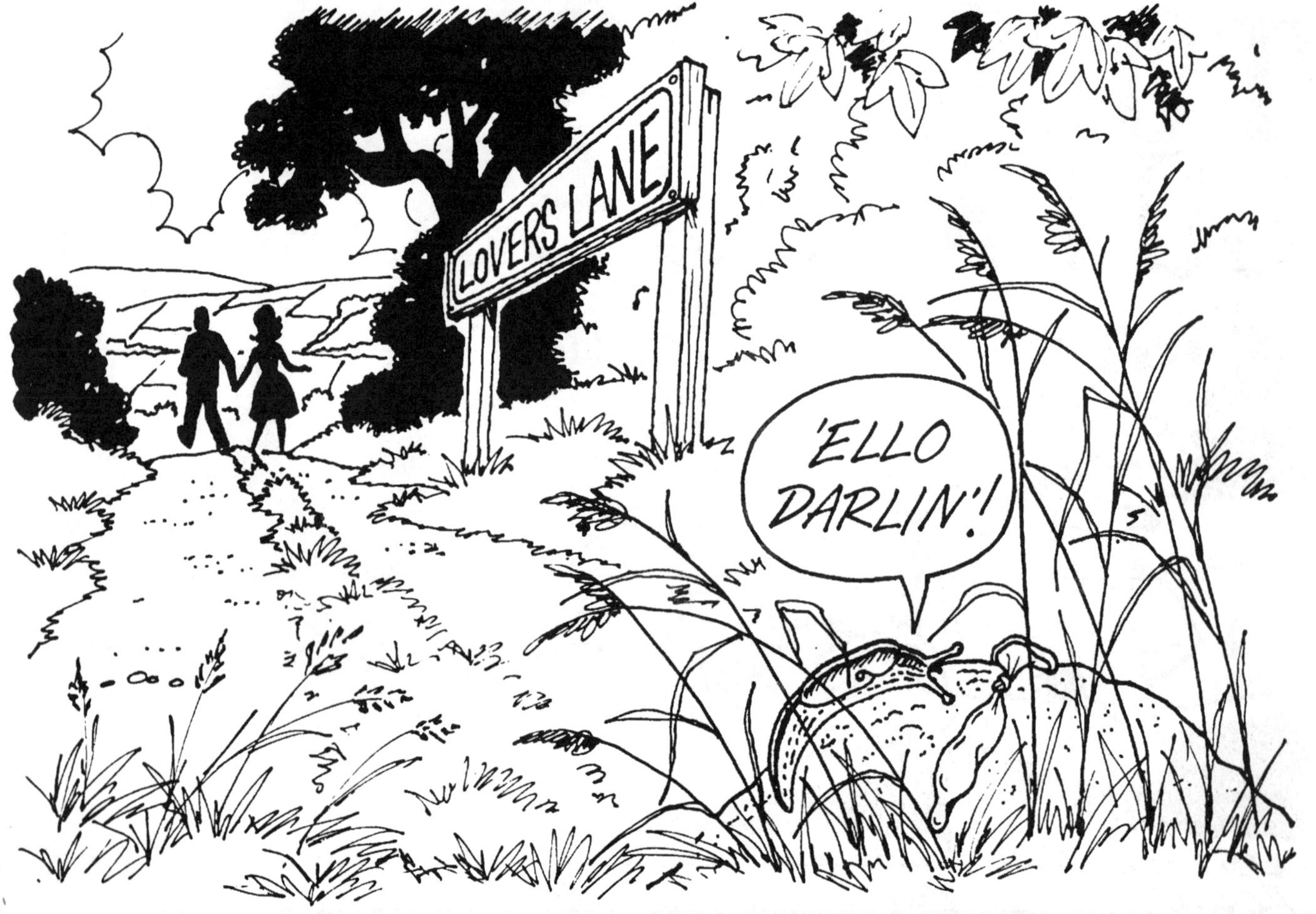
LOVERS LANE
'ELLO DARLIN'!

"JUST WAVE DEAR, HE'S PROBABLY THE VILLAGE IDIOT!"

"DON'T KNOW WHY WE BOTHERS PUTTING NOTICE UP FRANK! THE BUGGERS DON'T PAY NO HEED ANYHOW!"

"OH SIMON, AREN'T THEY CUTE WHEN THEY'VE BEEN SHEARED!"

"I DON'T MIND THE "REAL" ALE IN THESE PARTS, IT'S THE "REAL" CUSTOMERS THAT BOTHER ME!!"

"COME ON PEGGY LET'S GET A BUCKET OF WINKLES FOR LUNCH!"

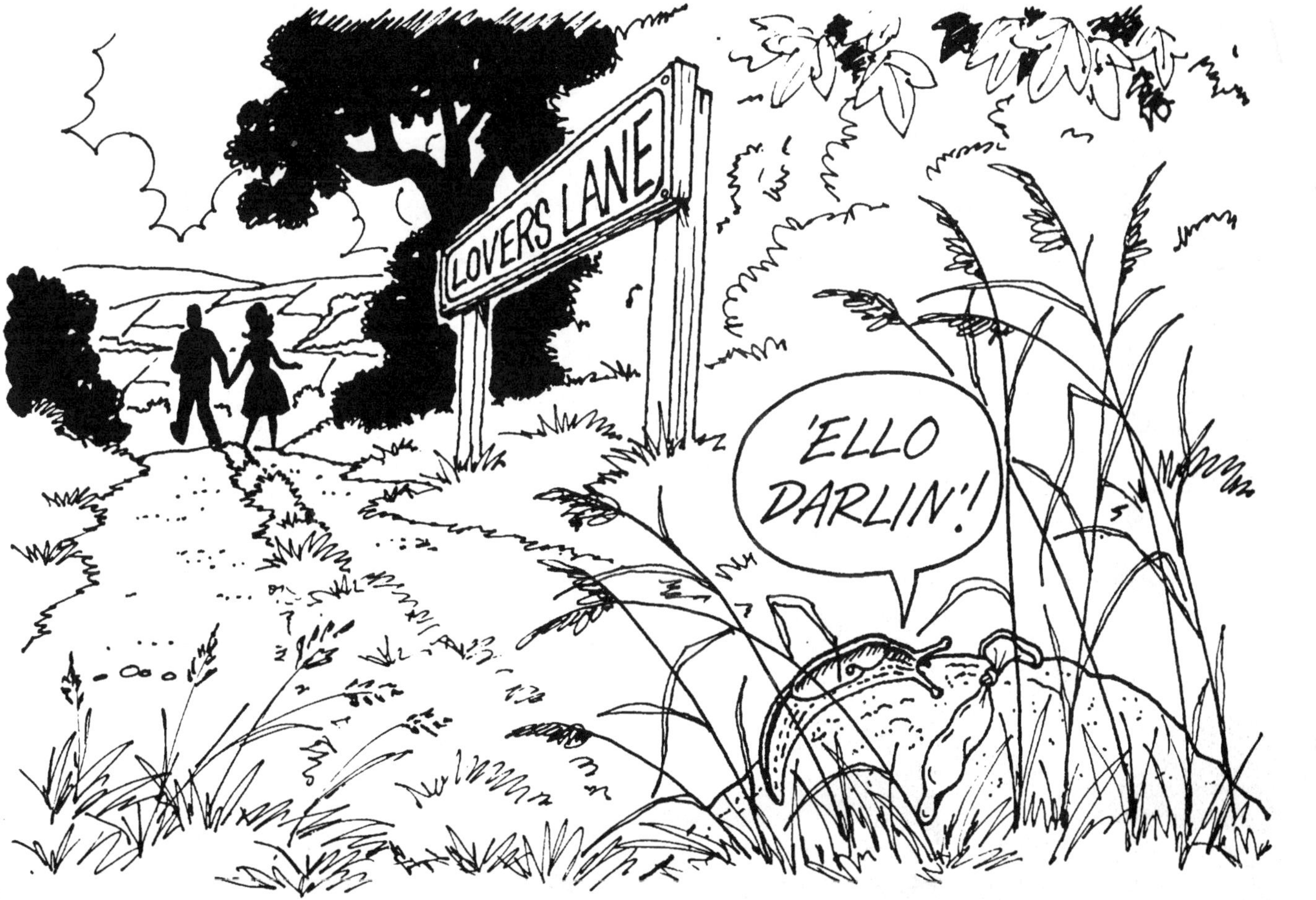

LOVERS LANE
'ELLO DARLIN'!

TOURISM & OUTWARD-BOUND...

"LISTEN PAL, WE MAY BE A BIT BEHIND THE TIMES 'ROUND HERE BUT NO, I AIN'T GOT CHANGE FOR A GROAT!"

"JUST WAVE DEAR, HE'S PROBABLY THE VILLAGE IDIOT!"

"AREN'T THEIR QUAINT OLD ACCENTS JUST SO CUTE!"

"I KNOW I CALLED YOU A BITCH AUDREY, BUT THERE'S NO NEED TO TAKE IT THIS FAR!"

"STICK YOUR PITON IN YON CREVICE DOUGIE!"

HUNTING SHOOTING & FISHING...

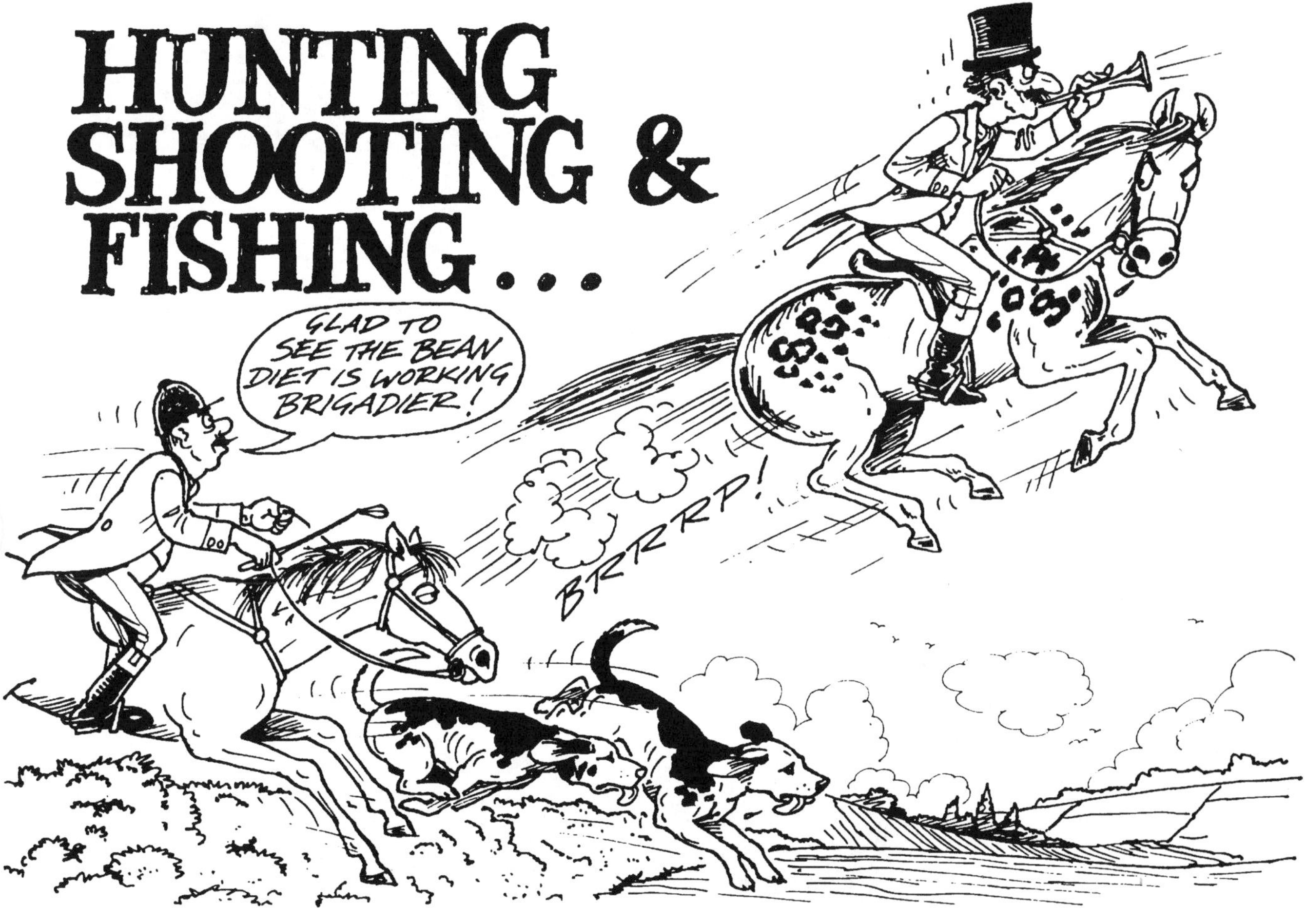

"'ERE MISTER 'E WON'T BITE YER WILL 'E?"
"NO SONNY, NOT ME WILLY, BUT 'E MIGHT STICK 'IS SNOUT UP MY ARSE LOOKIN' FER RABBITS!"
ROLL-UP!
20 pence agc
CHALLENG
HARRY TO
Ferrets down
TROUSERS!

"GOD HOW I WISH THE "GROUSE" SHOOTING SEASON WOULD START!"

"IT'S A BLOODY SHAME, ONE SEES SO LITTLE WILDLIFE ABOUT THESE DAYS!"

"YOU SAY HE SWALLOWED YOUR RIDING CROP MAJOR?... I CAN'T FEEL A THING IN THERE!

"I WISH THAT MAN WOULD GO AWAY. I'VE GOT TO G[ET] OUT SOON TO HIBERNATE!"

"DAMN YOU BUGLER, WE'VE GOT ENOUGH PROBLEMS WITH THIS LOT WITHOUT YOU STARTING THAT CROTCH-SNIFFING THING OF YOURS AGAIN!"

"THE COLONEL SAID IF WE WENT DOWN TO THE WOODS TODAY WE'D BE SURE OF A BIG SURPRISE!"

"THAT PARTY OF JUDGES IS BACK AT THE FISHING LODGE!"

"THAT'S WHAT HAPPENS TO NAUGHTY FOXES WHO DON'T WASH THEIR SCENT GLANDS EVERY DAY!"

ANTICIPATION!
SPLUTTER! WEEP!
"OH! STOP BLUBBING REGGIE! I TOLD YOU I'D TAKE YOU PIKE FISHING DIDN'T I?"

"IT WAS GOOD OF OLD HARRY TO LEAVE HIS BODY TO THE CLUB LADS!"

"I DON'T KNOW WHAT YOU SEE IN THEM TREVOR, THEY'RE SO UGLY!"

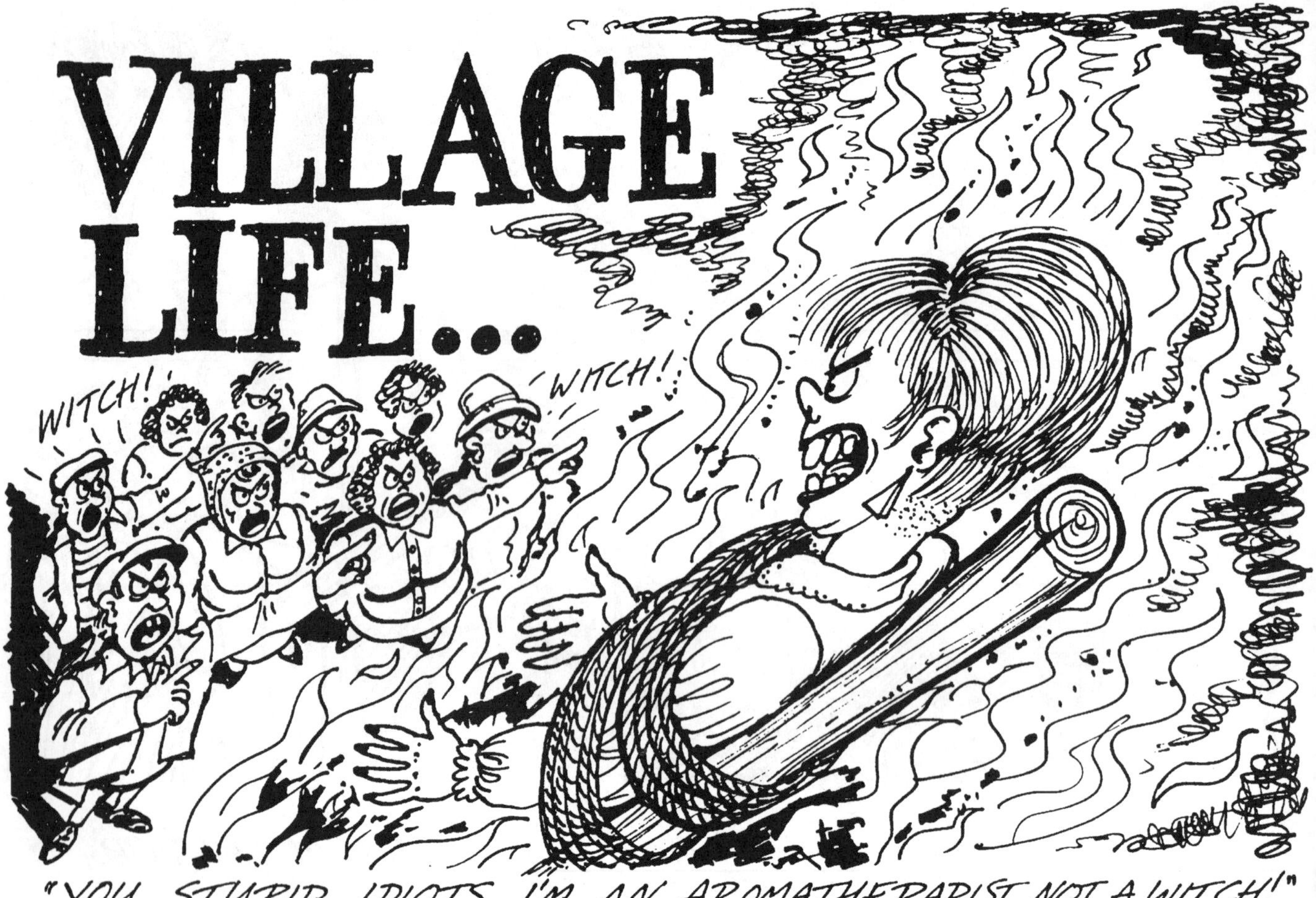

"YOU STUPID IDIOTS, I'M AN AROMATHERAPIST, NOT A WITCH!"

"HAPPENS EVERY YEAR SARGE, ONE OF 'EM TRYS TO BUY A JAM SPONGE WITH BUTTERCREAM ICING BEFORE THE FETE IS OFFICIALLY OPENED!"

"I SEE THIS SEASON'S SCRUMPY GETS 'EM JUST AS LEGLESS AS EVER!"

"GREAT IDEA CHARLIE TO GET THEM HOOKED ON CIGARETTES..
...THEY SAY REAL PEOPLE ARE JUST AS STUPID!"

YES READER, LITTLE PUDDLEWICK IN THE MARSH IS IN *DEEP* COUNTRY!

"WELCOME EVERYBODY, I HOPE YOU'RE ALL GOING TO ENJOY MY TALK ON AROMATHERAPY AS MUCH - ER - AS MUCH AS - PHEW - I AM!"

THE W.I. TALK ON BATS WAS NOT A SUCCESS!

"I'M SORRY BUT THE DOCTOR SAY I'VE GOT TO APPLY THIS TO MY RECTOR TWICE A DAY!"

"FOR F***'S SAKE MERVYN!"

"I DON'T WANTS ONE OF YOUR INDOOR TOILETS MISTER. OUT HERE THE WIND BLOWS THE STINK AWAY!"

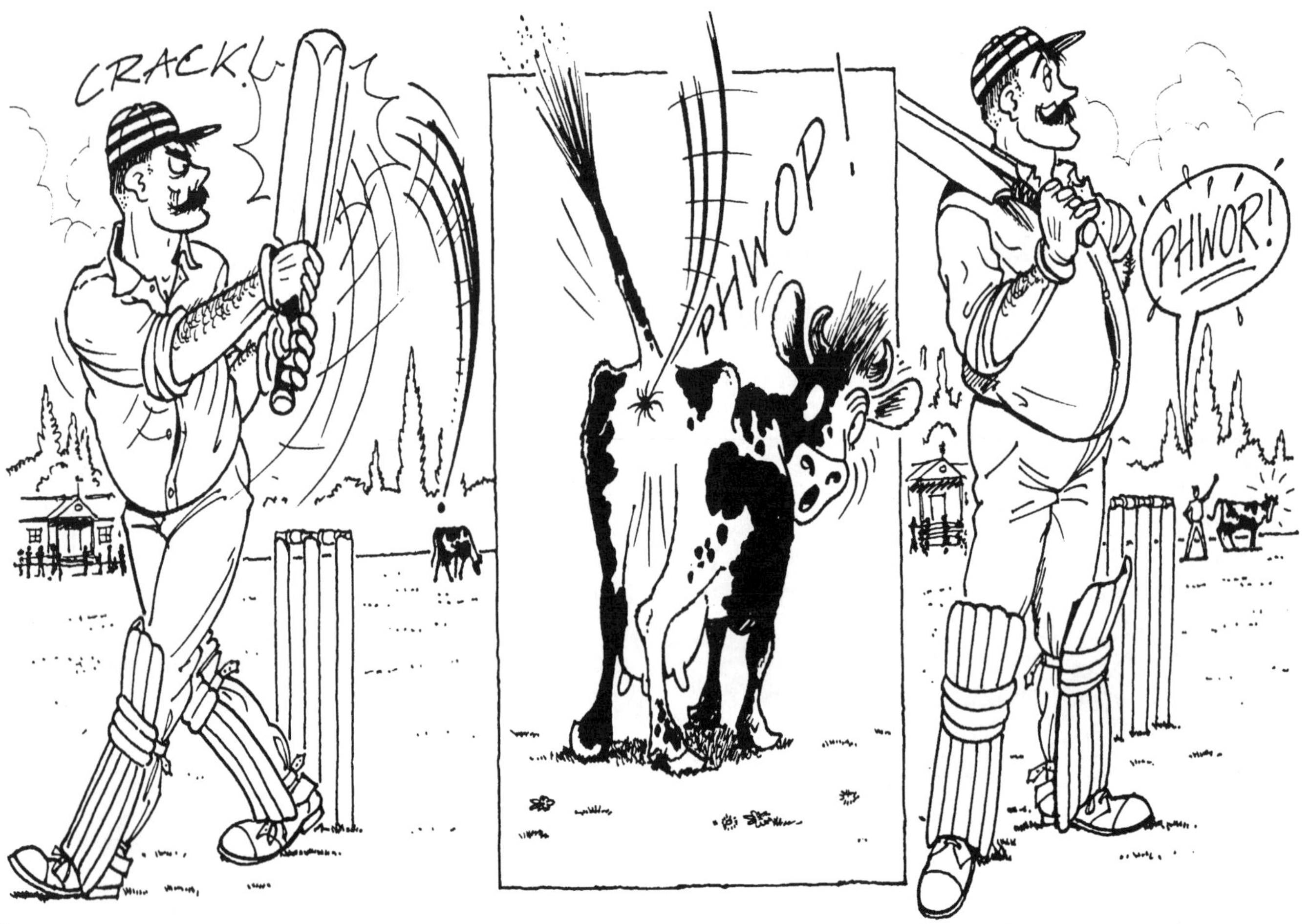
CRACK!
PHWOP!
PHWOR!

"I SEE YOUR WIFE'S STILL AWAY VICAR!"

TITLES BY POWERFRESH
· NORTHAMPTON · ENGLAND ·

Please Send Me:

CRINKLED 'N' WRINKLED	£2.99	[ ]
DRIVEN CRAZY	£2.99	[ ]
OH NO ITS XMAS AGAIN	£2.99	[ ]
TRUE LOVE	£2.99	[ ]
IT'S A BOY	£2.99	[ ]
IT'S A GIRL	£2.99	[ ]
NOW WE ARE 40	£2.99	[ ]
FUNNY SIDE OF 30s	£2.99	[ ]
FUNNY SIDE OF 40 HIM	£2.99	[ ]
FUNNY SIDE OF 40 HER	£2.99	[ ]
FUNNY SIDE OF 50 HIM	£2.99	[ ]
FUNNY SIDE OF 50 HER	£2.99	[ ]
FUNNY SIDE OF 60'S	£2.99	[ ]
FUNNY SIDE OF SEX	£2.99	[ ]
THE COMPLETE BASTARDS GUIDE TO GOLF	£2.99	[ ]
SEX IS...	£2.99	[ ]
FOOTNOTES	£2.99	[ ]
SPLAT	£2.99	[ ]
WE'RE GETTING MARRIED	£2.99	[ ]
THE ART OF SLOBOLOGY	£2.99	[ ]
THE DEFINITIVE GUIDE TO VASECTOMY	£2.99	[ ]
KEEP FIT WITH YOUR CAT	£2.99	[ ]
MARITAL BLISS AND OTHER OXYMORONS	£2.99	[ ]
THE OFFICE FROM HELL	£2.99	[ ]
PMT CRAZED	£2.99	[ ]
SEXY CROTCHWORD PUZZLES	£2.99	[ ]
STONED AGE MAN	£2.99	[ ]
OUT TO LUNCH	£2.99	[ ]
HORNY MAN'S ADULT DOODLE BOOK	£2.50	[ ]
HORNY GIRL'S ADULT DOODLE BOOK	£2.50	[ ]
IF BABIES COULD TALK	£2.99	[ ]
CAT CRAZY	£2.99	[ ]
MAD TO TRAVEL BY AIR...	£2.99	[ ]
MAD TO PLAY GOLF...	£2.99	[ ]
MAD TO HAVE A BABY...	£2.99	[ ]
MAD TO GET MARRIED...	£2.99	[ ]
BUT IT HELPS.		

I have enclosed cheque / postal order for £ .... made payable to **GUNNERS**

NAME...ADDRESS...

....

COUNTY..POSTCODE...

Please return to: Powerfresh Ltd. 3 Gray Street, Northampton, NN1 3QQ, ENGLAND.
EEC countries add £1 Postage, Packaging & Order processing. Outside EEC please add £3.00